CHOOSING & USI

Curtains
and Blinds

House Beautiful

CHOOSING & USING
Curtains
and Blinds

Carole Whittaker

TED SMART

A TED SMART Publication 1995
1 3 5 7 9 10 8 6 4 2

First published in 1995 by Ebury Press,
Random House, 20 Vauxhall Bridge
Road, London SW1V 2SA

Random House Australia (Pty) Limited,
20 Alfred Street, Milsons Point,
Sydney,New South Wales 2061,
Australia

Random House New Zealand Limited
18 Poland Road, Glenfield,
Auckland 10, New Zealand

Random House South Africa (Pty)
Limited PO Box 337, Bergvlei,
South Africa

Random House UK Limited
Reg. No. 954009A

CIP catalogue record for this book is
available from the British Library.
ISBN 009 180484 1

Editor: Emma Callery
Designed by Jerry Goldie Graphic
Design London

Colour separations by HBM Print Ltd

Printed and bound in Singapore
by Tien Wah Press

CONTENTS

INTRODUCTION

Welcome to our *Choosing and Using* series of practical books. Every home-owner knows the problems that so often go with the pride in creating a comfortable and attractive place to live. So with this in mind, our clear guides have been created to form a useful and inspirational series to keep on hand while you choose and use the essential elements for every room. With *Curtains and Blinds*, for example, we give you the ideas and know-how for making the most of windows anywhere, ranging from simple unlined curtains to more complex festoon blinds.

The other books in the series cover aspects in an equally detailed way and I know you'll find each book as useful and inspiring as every issue of House Beautiful magazine.

Pat Roberts Cairns

Pat Roberts Cairns
Editor

Left *Matching florals give a romantic feel to this room. Add detail with a decorative edged blind and iron forged pole.*

CHOOSING CURTAINS AND BLINDS

Curtains and blinds are expensive whether you make them yourself or not. They are most definitely a major investment so make sure you take some time to consider all the options to avoid a costly mistake.

Generally speaking, the more elaborate the design of the window dressing, the more fabric it will require and the more expensive it will be to make. Standard headed curtains will obviously use far less fabric than heavily pleated ones, just as a roman blind will be cheaper to make than a festoon blind.

However tight your budget may be, try to use fabric generously. Do not skimp on fabric to save money. It is better to use more of a less expensive fabric, as a better result will be obtained than using less of an expensive fabric. Spending a lot of money on fabric does not always guarantee success. Inexpensive fabrics such as calico and muslin can be draped and tied to look just as lavish as more expensive fabrics.

If your budget is very tight and you have some sewing skills then make your own curtains. If you have a moderate budget consider ready-mades and if you can afford to spend your money, then go for the luxury of made-to-measure curtains.

Right *Bold prints and colours can be mixed and matched very successfully. Here a bold check gives definition to an overall floral effect.*

SELECTING A STYLE

Choosing the right style of window dressing involves several major considerations. Shape and size of the window; its position in a room and the direction in which it faces; the function of the room, and the style and period of your home are all factors that must be taken into account. Equally, so must your personal tastes, preferences and budget.

PERSONAL STYLE

Style is very much a reflection of your own personality and therefore the choice of style you make will say a lot about you and your general outlook on life.

The secret of style is to have faith in your own taste. Many people are somewhat daunted by the prospect of making choices based on taste and style. Confidence is really the key, so take some time to think about what it is you really do like. Beware of following fashions blindly or making decisions based on other people's preferences. Bear in mind that it is you who will be living with your decor and not your friends, relatives and neighbours.

Make a design board from a large piece of card and stick cuttings from magazines, fabric swatches, paint cards, in fact anything that attracts your eye, on to it. You'll soon find that you hit on a style that is right for you, be it a contemporary modern look with natural materials such as unbleached textures and wood or a more elaborate traditional approach with florals and chintz.

You will soon start to

Above *Understated style in the form of a crisp white cut-work café curtain adds interest and privacy to an otherwise dull view.*

recognize just what it is you do like and have a little more confidence in making design decisions. Look for inspiration all around you and do not be afraid to borrow good ideas when you see them. Once you have an idea of what you actually like then apply these ideas to the house and room in question. Be prepared to be flexible; yes, you would love elaborate drapes in a heavenly chintz, but they may not totally suit the window or room in question.

Left *Flower festooned chintz is not to everyone's taste, but it can give a very luxurious feel to a bedroom.*

DISCOVERING YOUR STYLE

❖ Find a large piece of card to use as a design board.

❖ Pin your favourite magazine cuttings, fabric swatches and colours to it.

❖ Stand back and assess your taste.

❖ Hold on to the swatches and colours and keep them handy on shopping trips - they will be invaluable when choosing fabrics.

COLOUR, PATTERN AND TEXTURE

To a certain extent, colour, pattern and texture are a matter of personal preference. So, again, follow your own tastes and preferences and not others.

COLOUR

Colour plays a large part in decorating and can drastically change the mood and character of a room. Generally speaking, reds give a dramatic and dominant effect, blues give a cool and fresh look, greens are restful, yellows are sunny and warm, and pastels give a light and airy feel. For example, a dark and cold north facing room could be given a kiss of summer sunshine with a bright yellow or made warm and cosy with a bold red or orange.

PATTERN

Fabric is a very important way of adding colour and should be used to bring together the general decorating scheme of the room. Patterns are a good way of uniting several colours in a room scheme. A patterned fabric can be used to link a terracotta sofa with a midnight blue rug, for example. Checks and stripes which give a crisp look and can be used successfully in modern or traditional schemes, and florals look good in more formal and traditional design schemes.

If you decide on a bold pattern, bear in mind that you will need to take account of the pattern repeat when you come to measure up for your window dressing, or any matching soft furnishings you may wish to have.

Above Bright and cheerful patterns make roller blinds look something special.

TEXTURE

Another way of subtly introducing pattern into a scheme is by using textured fabrics. Texture can add tremendous depth and dimension to an otherwise flat and boring design scheme. Heavily textured ethnic weaves and crisp linens are two types of textured fabric which look great in any room. For a more traditional look consider rich damasks, glazed chintz, beautiful crewel work and, of course, lace.

Above Unlined curtains are very simple to make and neutral, sheer fabric will help to lighten an otherwise dark room.

PERIOD OF HOUSE

Above *A light and airy country feel with curtains and matching valance.*

The architectural style and period of your home will give you a good starting point as it is important to choose an appropriate style of window dressing. Is the house contemporary in style, built in the last 30-40 years? Or is it of an older period?

If you have an older house, you may wish to keep the window dressings in period. Research into relevant styles and fabrics by visiting your local library and consulting interior design books which illustrate designs of the period. Take a few sketches of suitable styles and make a note of the sorts of fabrics, trimmings and hardware used. Victorians, for example, were fond of elaborate drapes and pelmets in heavy fabrics such as velvet and brocade edged with fringing and tassels. Curtain poles with brass fittings were very much the order of the day.

To achieve a totally authentic look you would need to pay full reverence to the colours of the day too. Purples and greens were beloved of the Victorians.

Of course, not everyone wishes to feel they are living in another era, and contemporary window dressings can be applied successfully to a period home. Do try at all times, though, to be sympathetic to the original features.

The same applies to modern houses. Yes, swags and tails are elegant but do they really fit into a sixties' house? Try to be sympathetic to modern windows and choose a style that accentuates their good points and disguises their bad.

ROOM WITH A VIEW

Also consider the view from your window. Is the view dominated by glorious greenery or oppressive concrete? Would you like to preserve the view or hide it? Remember that your aim is to show off the window to its best advantage. If the view is less than attractive, and the room is light enough, consider a draped lace or voile blind. On the other hand, if the view is particularly beautiful, use your window dressing to frame the view.

Left *Cheerful blinds in bold fabrics make this loft room really stunning. They pull up high and out of the way to afford good views.*

FUNCTION OF ROOM

How you decide to dress your window will, to a certain extent, depend on what the room is used for. A bedroom window dressing, for example, will need to be private and well insulated and also afford a degree of luxury, while a kitchen will need a practical and easy to clean covering. To help you along the way to making the right choice for your room, here are some ideas for suitable window dressings for different rooms.

HALLS AND LANDINGS

First impressions are very important and the hall is the place in which you welcome your guests. Although you probably do not spend much time in the hall you do pass through it to reach other rooms in the house. Aim for a warm, welcoming and uncluttered look.

Halls and landings often have small feature windows which present problems when it comes to window dressing. If the window is not overlooked and is not too draughty, think about leaving it uncovered. Similarly the windows may be made from leaded lights and stained glass which give a degree of privacy without needing to add curtains or a blind. Where you do need to cover the window, go for a neat look that does not dominate its surroundings.

LIVING ROOMS

Living rooms can usually be split into two types, the family room, and the more formal sitting room. Family rooms need to be comfortable and practical. Curtains need to be easy to draw back and forth and not too precious, especially if you have a young family. Patterned fabric will hide a multitude of sins, go for a crisp check or tartan for a contemporary feel or an all over floral. If your children are still very young, play it safe and choose a fabric that is easily washable! A simple, full-length pair of drapes with a box pelmet would look attractive.

A more formal sitting room will require rather grander treatment and this is the room that you can really go to

Above A formal sitting room is the place to experiment with elaborate finishing touches such as swags and tails, rosettes and bows.

Left Pretty curtains lined with a contrasting fabric and teamed with a voile panel.

Above A corner of a room can become an elegant dining area. Formal curtains give a luxurious feel combined with an unusual fleur de lys blind.

town with. Full-length curtains with a swag pelmet and tiebacks would be the order of the day, perhaps in a rich silk or brocade.

DINING ROOMS

The dining room in most homes is a formal room used for entertaining dinner guests. As a result, the room is more often than not used in the evening. Remember that the curtains will therefore usually be seen fully drawn rather than open. A beautiful bold pattern may look good with tiebacks, but it could look a touch overpowering when drawn. That is not to say that you can't be bold with your overall design. Rich blues, golds and terracottas in brocades and velvets would look wonderful in a formal dining room, shown off to their best advantage by candlelight.

KITCHENS AND BREAKFAST ROOMS

Whatever you choose as a window dressing in these rooms will have to cope with steam, water, splashes of food and the general wear and tear that a kitchen gets. Make sure then, that the dressing is easy to clean, hard wearing and is kept well out of the way of work surfaces, sinks and cookers. For this reason blinds are a popular choice for kitchens. For a hi-tech look, choose a roller blind or venetian blind; for rustic charm, consider a split cane blind; for a softer look, add fabric in the shape of a roman blind.

If you have an adjoining breakfast room you could use the same fabric made up into a more elaborate dressing such as draped curtains with a valance, or an austrian blind.

Below A crisp and clean striped roller blind gives an uncluttered look to a small bathroom.

BATHROOMS

Privacy and insulation are important factors in a bathroom. Again, the window dressing will have to cope with steam and water and so must be easy to clean. If you have a large bathroom you will have the space to experiment with fabric, but if the space is small – and most bathrooms are – a clutter-free approach is preferable.

For a small-space bathroom, consider a cheerful beach hut look with a roller blind with a nautical feel. For a larger room, go for a more opulent style, perhaps full-length curtains or an elegant, ruched blind. Where space is really tight, create an illusion of space by using shutters backed with mirrors.

BEDROOMS

Aim for a mood of restfulness, peace and tranquillity. You can really go to town in a bedroom and indulge all your fantasies to create a 'dream' bedroom, be it a silk-covered boudoir or a flower-decked paradise. Because privacy is important in a bedroom, lace panels and sheer fabrics teamed with curtains, a pelmet and one or two finishing touches would be both practical and attractive. The room will need to be warm and cosy so always line bedroom curtains, and if the room is north facing, choose a thicker thermal lining and a generously gathered heading.

CHILDREN'S ROOMS

Again, practical considerations must be met. The room must be well insulated to keep your child warm and away from draughts. The window dressing must also exclude as much light as possible for day-time naps, so choose a blackout lining. Remember that children grow up very quickly so try to choose a style that will grow with them. Your bouncing baby boy will soon object to pastel frills and bows even if they are in blue! Blinds are particularly suitable for children's rooms, they take up little space and can be pulled up and away from tiny hands.

Above Split cane blinds are a smart and practical option for a child's room.

STUDIES AND WORKROOMS

An organized and uncluttered look is often the order of the day. Good light is essential and a means of filtering light may be required if the room is south facing. A venetian blind would be a good choice. Soften the harsh look with a wooden venetian or a cheap and cheerful split cane or more expensive pinoleum blind.

For a traditional study or library, choose a grander look with curtains, pelmet and perhaps a matching blind.

CONSERVATORIES

If your conservatory faces any direction other than north, you will almost certainly require some sort of shading. If you are a keen plants person, and like to be surrounded by greenery, you could grow your own natural blind. Climbers such as passion flower and jasmine will quickly do the job for you.

There are a wide variety of blinds on the market which are suitable for conservatories. Pinoleum blinds look attractive and have a very natural appearance in keeping with greenery. If your conservatory gets very hot, metallic-backed blinds are available which help deflect some of the heat. For a cheap and cheerful alternative to expensive made-to-measure blinds, use split cane blinds on the windows of the conservatory and drape muslin over wooden dowels to tent the roof. Remember that even in north facing conservatories the light will quickly fade fabrics.

Above *Blinds provide much needed shade in a conservatory and look very attractive too.*

PROPORTIONS OF ROOMS AND WINDOWS

Windows come in all shapes and sizes and it is up to you to try to make the most of what you have - try to enhance the best features and disguise the worst. Long, narrow windows, for example, will require a very different treatment from short, wide ones. Windows that are often opened will need window dressings that draw clear of the window. A pretty lace panel may look attractive on a sash window but will have to be lifted out of the way to give access to open the window.

FINE FEATURES

Not all windows need be dressed. A fine feature window will have enough style and interest to stand alone without embellishment. If you do need to cover a feature window for privacy, however, choose a plain, simple style that will pull back clear of the window. A plain cream fabric to match the window's framework would render the dressing invisible, serving practical requirements but remaining sympathetic to the window.

Common problems with window shapes and sizes and their positions in rooms crop up again and again. Here we list the most common window shapes and associated problems and give ideas on how to dress them.

BAY WINDOWS

Curved bays tend to present more design problems as they are usually wider than they are tall - see Short, wide windows opposite. In place of curtains, blinds and shutters can look equally good.

❖ Curtains look best if they hang inside the bay rather than across the front. A window seat is sometimes incorporated into a bay window which would rule out full-length curtains, as would a radiator, which is often sited under a bay window.

❖ If you are hanging curtains around the bay use a good quality track that will bend to fit the shape. A metal track would be strong enough to cope with heavily lined curtains, a plastic track would not. Similarly, corded tracks will put more pressure on the track. A heavy-duty track can be covered with

a pelmet or valance. Iron forged rods are very popular and can be fitted to bay windows, as can wooden curtain poles. However, to secure them correctly you will need extra supports and therefore four rather than two curtains.

SHORT, WIDE WINDOWS

Often found in modern houses where ceilings are lower, these windows may have very large panes of glass to give an unobstructed view. Blinds are well suited to modern windows but they do need to be softened with a little pattern, colour and texture. For this reason, roman blinds are an excellent choice as they bridge the gap between modern and traditional styles.

❖ To make the window look narrower, add gathered curtains which meet in the middle and are pulled back at the sides with tiebacks.

❖ To make the window look taller, add a pelmet or valance high above the track.

Left Lightweight sheers ensure one's eye is drawn to the window's fine features.

Above Disguise tall, narrow windows with curtains hung on poles that are wider than the window.

TALL, THIN WINDOWS

Most period town houses have long, thin windows designed to be in proportion with the high ceilings. These sort of windows can be very expensive to dress and usually require a formal style with curtains, blinds, pelmets and tiebacks. Experiment with cheaper fabrics like calico, muslin, dress linings and even parachute silk.

❖ If you wish to make the window look wider, extend the track or pole well beyond the window and add gathered curtains to create the illusion of width.

❖ If the window appears far too tall, add a deep pelmet, swag or valance to cover a large proportion of the curtain. This will help reduce the overall size of the window opening.

CIRCULAR, ARCHED AND OTHER FEATURE WINDOWS

Great care must be taken with feature windows - where possible, avoid covering them at all. Where you really to have to cover them, try incorporating their shape into the chosen covering.

❖ For an arched window use a pelmet to echo the shape of the arch and use it to hide a straight piece of track.

❖ A shutter, venetian blind or piece of sheer fabric will give privacy and help keep out draughts, but the shape of the window frame will still be partially visible.

DORMER WINDOWS AND SKYLIGHTS

Windows such as these add valuable light to an otherwise dark space and may give excellent views. Dormer windows usually have a deep recess and are relatively small for the size of room so try to allow as much as light as possible to come in.

❖ Swivel rod curtains are an ideal choice.
❖ Velux loft windows are often clothed in simple roller blinds, but you could experiment with other sorts of blinds for a softer look.

PATIO WINDOWS

By nature, patio windows are very large and may well cover the entire wall of a room. Obviously, the view is an important feature and so the window dressing should not obscure it in any way. Because of the size of the doors, any covering will require a lot of fabric and will need to cope with being the entrance from the garden.

❖ The doors will be opened and passed through regularly, so curtains should pull well back out of the way.
❖ Patio doors are usually double glazed but heavier curtains may still be needed in winter.

FRENCH WINDOWS

Full-length curtains are obviously required for french windows. Older style french windows can be very draughty and so good insulation is essential.

❖ Curtains should draw back well out of the way, held in place with tiebacks.
❖ Add a matching pelmet for a period feel.

Below *Elegant curtains make this kitchen eating area more formal and are pulled well back with tiebacks to allow access to the french windows.*

CURTAINS

Curtains are very much the traditional and popular choice for most windows. They are highly practical and yet can be used imaginatively to create a feeling of luxury and warmth. They can be used to create all sorts of optical illusions and help you to present the very best features of your window. Curtains can be used on their own or combined with blinds, pelmets and tiebacks. They can be hung from elaborate poles and many different types of heading can be used.

WHAT'S WHAT

Unlined curtains Not all curtains need to be lined. Indeed, some fabrics such as sheers and open weave and self-patterned fabrics look best when light is allowed to gently filter through them. Often fabrics like damasks can lose the definition of their pattern when they are unlined.

Left *A contrasting lining and imaginative detail heading adds great interest.*

Below *You needn't restrict yourself to lining curtains with a plain fabric. Here the lining contrasts most unconventionally.*

Lined curtains Linings come in three groups: separate linings, loose linings or locked-in linings. Separate linings can be bought and added to existing curtains, hanging from the same curtain hook. Loose linings, however, are the most common and popular way of lining curtains. Locked-in linings give a fine and highly professional touch, but they are time consuming and require a degree of patience and skill. There are a variety of weights and colours of lining available: thermal linings help cut out draughts and reduce fuel bills; blackout linings cut out all light.

Experiment with alternative lining materials such as gingham, ticking and calico, to give interest.

Interlining This is a layer of insulated material which is sewn between the curtains and lining, giving a rather grand - if bulky - look.

Ready-mades There is an enormous ready-made selection in the shops, ideal for creating instant window dressings. Matching pelmets, valances and tiebacks are also available, or you can give ready-mades greater individuality by adding your own personal touch with contrasting trimmings. Ready-mades are considerably cheaper than made-to-measure curtains and come in an ever increasing range of fabrics, headings and styles. They are quick and easy, can be bought off the shelf and put

Below *Interlining is used to give a very opulent look to a plain pair of curtains.*

up the same day without having the inconvenience and expense of having them made up.

Although there is now more choice than ever before, the range can still be limiting. Not everyone has standard size windows and in some cases made-to-measure may be the only solution. Ready-mades would be ideal for a bedroom window, for example, but an oddly shaped bay would require a little more thought.

Made-to-measure

The most expensive option of the three, made-to-measure curtains give a professional finish and offer total flexibility of choice of design and fabric. You are able to match fabrics and colours exactly and can have any design idea made up. They are also often the best answer for an awkward shaped window.

Interior design shops and larger stores will charge quite a lot for this service, but many will give you a free design consultation in your own home to discuss styles, fabrics and suitable hardware as well as measuring up your window. So although you will pay a lot, you will be getting a totally professional service.

On the other hand, by following the advice given in this book you can choose the style, fabric and hard-ware you prefer and then all that remains is for the curtains to be made up. Lessen the expense by measuring up and buying the fabric yourself (see pages 73 and 75), or get a curtain maker to measure up and tell you how much fabric to buy.

Find curtain makers' names in the telephone directory or ask around for a recommended name. Fabric studios and shops will often recommend someone they use.

Making your own

This is by far the cheapest option for window dressing and certainly the most satisfying. If you know how to use a sewing machine and have some basic skills you should be able to make a simple pair of unlined curtains (see page 46) and a simple roller blind (see page 60) to match. In the process you'll be saving yourself a lot of money.

There is also great satisfaction from knowing that your fabric costs next to nothing in a sale and that you made up those lovely curtains in a weekend. Admittedly, you do require plenty of space to lay out fabric, one or two tools and a room free from pets and small children. Most importantly of all, you need TIME. All that being said, this book should inspire you to have a go.

PRACTICAL POINTERS

❖ Ready-made curtains are ideal for standard windows.

❖ Made-to-measure curtains are the best option for a problem window.

❖ If your budget is tight, make your own.

❖ Ready-made curtains are much cheaper than made-to-measure curtains.

❖ Larger stores have ready-made curtains in fabrics to match their own cushions and bedding.

❖ They are also ideal for people with little spare time or no sewing skills.

❖ If making your own curtains, start with a simple project.

❖ Enrol in an evening class to brush up your skills.

HEADINGS

Your choice of heading will depend on the effect you wish to achieve and your budget, as some headings require more fabric than others. Before you go out and buy your fabric, you will therefore need to decide on the type of heading you want for your curtains. The heading is an important design feature so do not just go out and buy standard headed tape before examining all the possibilities. At the same time, you will have to give some thought to the type of track, pole or rod you want as this is crucial to the style, size and weight of the curtains.

TAPED HEADINGS

These are the means by which fabric is gathered up and attached to a track, pole or rod and are the most conventional choice for curtains. The tapes have tabs in which to insert curtain hooks which then can be hooked on to the appropriate hardware. Tapes give different degrees and styles of gathers to the curtain and will determine if it is crisply pleated or gently gathered.

ALTERNATIVE HEADINGS

Less conventional headings are now very popular and are even available in ready-made form, including ties, bows, loops and casing. Hardware (see pages 32-5) can be used to increase the range to include clip-on headings, hooked headings, and curtain ring headings. In fact, the possibilities are endless.

WHAT'S WHAT

Standard tape This gives a gently gathered look, and requires a fullness of $1\frac{1}{2}$ times the track width.

Pencil pleat tape This forms a much deeper, formal look. Allow $2\frac{1}{4}$ times the track width. Mini-pencil pleats are available for short or lightweight curtains.

Pinch pleat tape Gathered into triple or double pleats, this tape looks very attractive in a traditional setting. It tends to be quite greedy with fabric, requiring $2\frac{1}{2}$ times the track width.

Box pleats These are wide and flat and make smart pelmets as well as

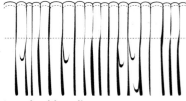

Standard heading

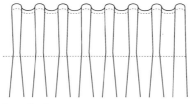

Pencil pleats

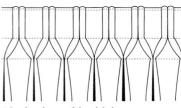

Pinch pleats (double)

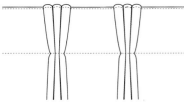

Pinch pleats (triple)

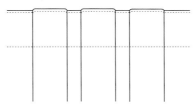

Box pleats

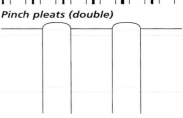

Cartridge pleats

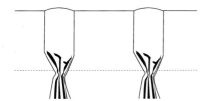

Goblet pleats

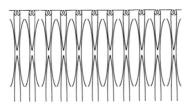

Lattice pleats

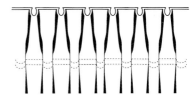

Trellis pleats

curtain headings and require at least double the track width.

Cartridge pleats
Cylindrical and effective in a modern setting, allow twice the track width for fabric for this style of heading.

Goblet pleats
These pleats are cartridge pleats which are secured by a stitch at the base and give a very traditional look.

Lattice pleats
With this heading, an alternating series of long and short pencil pleats is created which would be ideal for a valance.

It requires 2-2½ times the track width.

Trellis pleats
These are an attractive variation on pencil pleat and require 1½ -2 times the track width.

Bows, ties and loop headings
These can be made in matching or contrasting fabric or trimmings, and are very easy to make but may be less practical to draw.

Casing headings
Here is a heading that is very easy to make and cuts down on the amount of fabric required. Simply

create an open-ended hem at the top of the curtain and slot through the curtain pole.

Clip-on rings
Likewise, these also cut down on fabric requirements. They operate by clipping on to the top edge of the fabric. The ring is then threaded on to a pole or rod.

Curtain rings
These rings are a traditional method of hanging curtains which still look good today. Rings are sewn on at intervals to the top edge of the fabric and threaded on to a curtain pole or rod.

HARDWARE

Tracks, poles and rods are available in a bewilderingly large range. Choose one that will suit your curtain design and heading - or make sure that the heading fits the hardware if you have chosen that first.

Usually available in wood or brass, poles come in a variety of widths, which can be fitted to metal or wooden supports. The new breed of poles and rods come with elaborate finials and matching holdbacks in virtually any shape and size. Curtain rings are threaded on to the pole or rod and the curtains are attached by way of hooks through eyelets or clips on to the rings.

Track systems are available in plastic and aluminium and come corded or uncorded. The way your curtains are hung will very much determine how they look. Do not pay hundreds of pounds on beautiful made-to-measure curtains simply to hang them on your existing plastic track, take a look at all the options.

WHAT'S WHAT

Wood poles A vast range of wood finishes are available from natural, to paint or varnish yourself, to richly polished mahogany.

Metal poles These are available in a variety of forms from brass and chrome to iron forged rods. They are easy to fit, sturdy, and look very attractive in a wide variety of settings from traditional to modern.

Plastic tracks Generally speaking, the plastic tracks are the cheaper option and would be most suitable for a standard size and shape of window with lightweight curtains.

Metal tracks These are usually made from aluminium and are suitable for larger windows with perhaps a bay. Aluminium tracks usually come in white but a coloured range including a brass colour is available.

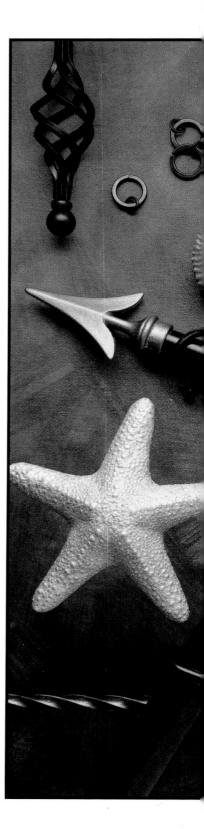

❖ Always make sure your track will bear the weight of the chosen style of curtains.

❖ Poles and rods around bay windows are available but make sure there is adequate support for the weight of curtain. To allow this you may have to have four rather than two curtains in a bay.

❖ When measuring a curved pole for a bay, remember to measure the shape where the pole should be and not the window.

❖ Get a local blacksmith to make you an iron forged rod at a fraction of the price of a shop bought one.

❖ A cheap idea for a small window would be a wooden mop handle cut to size and mounted on iron mounts.

❖ Casing headings can be threaded directly on to a pole or rod.

Left Just a small selection of the inspirational range of hardware now available.

Valance tracks Very versatile, these can either be used on their own or as part of a curtain and valance dual track.

Corded tracks Corded systems allow for easy curtain pulling. The more expensive models have pulleys at one or both sides to draw or open the curtains. Tracks are highly sophisticated these days and there is even a remote control model on the market that can be operated on a time switch as a security device. This system would also be a good option for an elderly or disabled person.

Below A wide range of hardware accessories are now available to make curtain making and hanging much more professional.

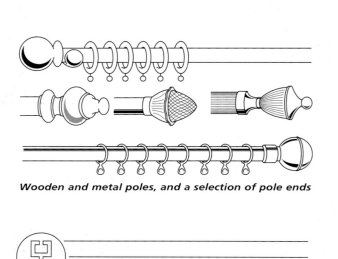

Wooden and metal poles, and a selection of pole ends

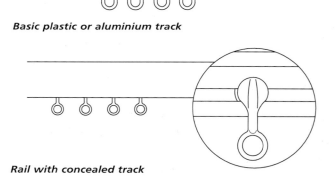

Basic plastic or aluminium track

Rail with concealed track

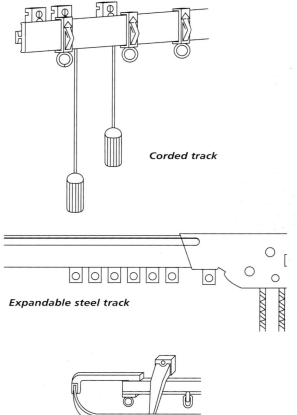

Corded track

Expandable steel track

Combined track and valance rail

HOLDBACKS

Holdbacks are hard tiebacks which usually match the new range of poles and rods. They serve the same function as tiebacks (see page 38) but are solid and are usually made from wood, or metal. Holdbacks are very practical and easy to fix, enabling you to drape curtains attractively. They are screwed on to a wall on either side of the window and the curtains are hooked back behind them. They are particularly useful for heavyweight curtains.

❖ Have a go at making your own finials and holdbacks using, say, cardboard cut to shape and covered with fabric, decorative paper, or sprayed with paint.

❖ Buy plain wooden holdbacks and customize them - gold sprayed starfish or ceramic plaques would look good.

SWAG HOLDERS

A range of hooks, rings and clips are available which are attached to the rod, pole or wall to hold a drape of fabric. They are ideal for creating instant swags and tails.

❖ Swag holders are a very simple way of creating a sophisticated finishing touch for your windows.

❖ They can be attached to the pole or track if you don't want to drill into walls.

Above *Beautifully finished iron forged holdbacks match poles and finials and look great in both modern and traditional settings.*

PRACTICAL POINTERS

❖ If you require a heavy metal track with a number of bends, consider getting it professionally fitted.

❖ Make sure that the track you choose is strong enough for the weight of window dressing.

❖ Spray cords and track with anti-static spray for an easy gliding track.

❖ Bend plastic tracks into shape with a hair dryer.

PELMETS

Pelmets help to frame a window – which is particularly good if there is a good view outside – and they add a touch of class to an otherwise ordinary pair of curtains. They can also be used to good effect to disguise the size and shape of a window and to give a neat finish to the top of the curtains. Just as at home in a cosy cottage as a Georgian mansion, pelmets are very adaptable and there is a wide variety on the market. If used in the shape of swags and tails, they give a period touch to an elegant town house.

The main purpose of the pelmet is to cover the top of a curtain and give a neat finish. The depth and shape of the pelmet will depend on the shape and size of the window and the effect you wish to achieve.

WHAT'S WHAT

Hard (or box) pelmet This is the simplest type of pelmet and is usually made from wood which is then painted, stained or covered with fabric for a softer look.

Valances These are the soft option in the choice of pelmets and are softly gathered or frilled skirts which fit across the top of the window to hide the tracking. They are usually fitted on to their own track. They can be used to add a special finishing touch but try to control the frilly look. You can choose from straight edge or curved valances.

Below A painted wooden pelmet provides the perfect foil to chintz roses.

Swags and tails Best described as an elaborate valance, the swag is a fabric drape which is fixed across the top of the window. The tails are tailored and hang on either side of the window and they are usually lined with a contrasting fabric. On page 52, we show you how to make simple swags and tails involving little or no sewing.

PRACTICAL POINTERS

❖ Use a pelmet to improve the proportions of your window. A deep pelmet, for example, will help make a very long, narrow window look shorter.

❖ Use a patterned pelmet to tie in other colours in your room scheme.

❖ A pelmet will give a neat and elegant finish to an otherwise plain pair of curtains.

Above *A grand pelmet makes the rather ordinary window something special.*

TIEBACKS AND TRIMMINGS

Tiebacks are available in a wide variety of materials from fabric to cording. They help your curtains drape well and frame the window they dress. They are attached to hooks on the wall and loop around the curtain to pull it back very neatly. High street stores have ready-made tiebacks and DIY kits to suit every imaginable style. They can be very simple to make and are ideal for the beginner. Tiebacks use very little fabric and if you are feeling creative the possibilities are endless. Improvise with scarves, beads, belts or try making your own from scratch.

Above A simple length of ribbon with fringed ends gives a jaunty look to a checked curtain.

WHAT'S WHAT

Fabric Tiebacks made from fabric come in the form of plaits, bows and - most commonly - stiffened fabric, in a variety of shapes. They can be easily made from remnants of fabric to match curtains and cushions.

Cord These tiebacks come in a wide range of colours and materials from elegant satin ones to natural 'rope'. Generally they are bought ready-made but you could have a go at making your own.

PRACTICAL POINTERS

❖ Use braids and fringing to give definition to a plain pelmet.

❖ Braids, fringing and ribbon can be stuck on instead of sewn. Use a good quality glue.

Right Exquisite examples of fringing, cord and tassels made from richly coloured chenille. Experiment yourself with chenille knitting yarns.

TRIMMINGS

Added details can make all the difference to the finished effect, so make the extra effort to incorporate a little something. Braids, fringing, edging - they can be used to give a totally individual finish to your window dressings. They are a particularly good way to add verve to an old pair of ready-made curtains too.

WHAT'S WHAT

Braids and ribbons
These are woven lengths of fabric sold in a variety of finishes and textures which can be used to give decorative touches.

Fringing
This gives an elaborate finish to curtains and pelmets. It usually comes ready-made, but even-weave fabrics can be fringed.

Fabric
Edgings made from fabric can be used to add interest to plain curtains.

Tassels and cords
These plaited and twisted yarns work well as tiebacks or decoration for valances, pelmets and curtain headings.

Bias binding
Binding comes in the form of strips of fabric cut on the cross and is used to edge curtains and pelmets. It is also used to cover piping cord to give a decorative edging.

BLINDS

Not only do blinds come in all shapes and sizes, they are also available in a very wide range of materials which makes them an extremely versatile window dressing. Paper, plastic, metal, wood, fabric and cane can all be used to make blinds. Their clean lines fit in equally well with modern or traditional schemes and a pelmet or valance can be added to give a softer look. For the full works, blinds are often combined with curtains.

WHAT'S WHAT

Roller blinds Simple, neat and usually inexpensive, roller blinds are easy to make and many excellent kits are on the market at a very low cost. They are usually made-to-measure but ready-mades are available which can be cut down to fit your window exactly. A spring mechanism controls and fixes the position of the blind and the stiffened fabric rolls up neatly when not in use. A cord pull is fixed at the bottom of the blind.

Although these blinds are neat they can look a little austere and are therefore often used to create a rather minimalistic look. Popular in small rooms where they don't take up too much room, they are particularly good for kitchens and bathrooms when made up in a water resistant fabric that is washable.

For a more opulent look they can be teamed with curtains and pelmets to give a fine finish. This is especially practical where they are teamed with fixed curtains which are never drawn. Curtains can be made to look very expensive in this way, but lots of fabric can be saved by using the roller blind to give the privacy. A plain roller blind can be given a new look with a pattern or texture or perhaps a decorative edging.

Roman blinds These are a more formal window treatment and give a very neat, crisp and contemporary feel to a room. They are worked by pulling vertical cords which cause the blind to double back on itself in a number of folds.

Above *Roller blinds can really be made to look special. A glorious fabric and interesting decorative edging makes all the difference.*

Austrian blinds

These are ruched blinds trimmed with a frill. Tapes running vertically are pulled to cause the blind to gather into ruches. When the blind is lowered, the ruches unfold to give a flat blind.

Festoon blinds
For a very ornate window dressing, use a festoon blind which is ruched both vertically and horizontally to give a very full blind. Revived from Victorian times, they are very popular and look good in a romantic bedroom. When the blind is down it will retain its ruches and fullness.

Pinoleum blinds

Fitting very well into the

Above *Ruched blinds made up in understated light and neutral fabrics will always look stunning.*

natural decor of the nineties, pinoleum blinds are made from pieces of wood woven together and edged with cotton tape. They are well made and very attractive and so naturally rather expensive.

PRACTICAL POINTERS

❖ Roller blinds are easy to make and give a neat finish to a window.

❖ Roller blinds also require very little fabric.

❖ For festoon blinds choose a lightweight fabric, otherwise the blind may look rather heavy.

❖ When making austrian and festoon blinds, use the special tapes which are available for the ruching.

Pinoleum blinds operate in the same way as roller blinds and some work like roman blinds. They give a lovely diffused light and are therefore a favourite for conservatories. Available in natural finish or a range of colours.

Split cane blinds
A cheaper option than pinoleum blinds, split cane blinds nevertheless give a similar effect. Made from lengths of split cane woven together, they work like roller blinds and so can be a little bulky when rolled up. They can be varied by adding a contrasting fabric edging.

Venetian blinds
Horizontal slatted blinds come in a variety of materials from metal to plastic and - most fashionably - wood. They are available in a large range of colours and some companies will spray them to match your own decor. A cord or rod is used to adjust the angle of the slats, thus allowing exactly the right amount of light into the room. Generally expensive as they are made to measure, they are worth every penny.

Vertical blinds
These come in easy-to-clean materials with interesting textures and the vertical slats can be adjusted to give the right amount of light.

Pleated blinds
These are very inexpensive and are available in a range of colours and materials, but are most often made from paper.

Shutters
Although often found in old houses, for a contemporary choice choose shutters. Slatted shutters give a rather colonial look to a room.

Left Pleated blinds may be cheap and cheerful but they needn't look it. This blind fits very well into its luxurious surrounds.

Right Painted to match the window frame, these shutters give privacy but in no way detract from the features of the window.

USING CURTAINS AND BLINDS

In this section we take a detailed look at making curtains - both unlined and lined - and all their accessories from pelmets and valances to tiebacks and rosettes and bows; and then we move on to making blinds. Where curtains are purely decorative or only dress curtains, blinds can become the practical window covering. From neat, sleek roller blinds to glorious, frilled austrian blinds, blinds are becoming an increasingly popular way of dressing a window. They are quite often a cheaper option than curtains and therefore suit those on a tight budget. So, whether you want to make a simple unlined curtain or a more complicated festoon blind, the instructions are given here in simple, step-by-step form.

If you want to have a go, but haven't made curtains or blinds before, begin with a simple project: do not launch into elaborate and heavy, fully-lined curtains for your sitting room. If they do not turn out right first time, you will have made a very expensive mistake that will probably put you off curtain making for life! Take one step at a time – perhaps you have a small bathroom window you could start with. Before plunging in, however, look at pages 72-5 for some good practical sewing tips.

Right *Simple curtains are pulled back to give a theatrical look and finished off with a matching rosette.*

MAKING UNLINED CURTAINS

Where privacy and warmth are not an issue, why not leave your curtains unlined? Often light and airy and not involving any complicated sewing techniques, unlined curtains are a perfect choice for the beginner to make.

WHAT TO DO

YOU WILL NEED

Fabric

Thread

Weights (optional)

Headed tape

Hooks

Tools of the trade

1 Follow the measuring up and fabric calculation instructions on page 73.

2 Cut the fabric to the right size, joining widths of fabric where required. Many curtains for smaller windows only require one width of fabric per curtain. Where you do need to join widths do so with a flat seam (see page 74) with a 12mm ($^1/_2$in) allowance. Cut notches along the selvedges at 15cm (6in) intervals. Press seams open.

3 Turn in and press 5cm (2in) on each side edge. Make a double 2.5cm (1in) hem. Pin, and tack to within 6.5cm (2$^1/_2$in) of the top edge and 15cm (6in) of the lower edge.

4 Turn up and press 15cm (6in) along the lower edge.

5 Press a mitre at each corner (see page 74) and turn in the raw edges to make a double 7.5cm (3in) hem.

6 Machine stitch the side turnings, or hand sew them for a more professional finish.

7 To weight curtains, pop weights into the hem before stitching the mitres and bottom hem.

8 Turn down and press 6.5cm (2$^1/_2$in) along the top of the curtain.

9 Cut heading tape to the width of the curtain plus 5cm (2in) for turnings. Pull out about 2.5cm (1in) of the cord at each end of the tape. Knot the cords together. Pin and sew in place.

10 Pull cords at the end of the curtain that will be at the wall edge until the gathering is as you desire. Tie the cords and tuck them out of sight. Insert hooks at 7.5cm (3in) intervals along the tape.

BRIGHT IDEAS FOR SIMPLE CURTAINS

❖ Make tie-on headings in pretty gingham ribbon to breath life into a tired old pair of curtains.

❖ Clip curtain rings on to a patchwork quilt or unusual table cloth to give a totally unique curtain. When you want a change, simply unclip and find a new piece of fabric.

❖ Make no-sew curtains by simply draping fabric over a pole or rod. Use a blind to give the privacy you require.

Left *Unlined curtains are very simple to make and, with light streaming through the fabric, can enhance the overall look.*

MAKING LINED CURTAINS

Not all curtains need to be lined but generally they do look and hang better if they are. You could break away from traditional linings and try lining curtains with a coordinating lining, even making the curtains reversible. Check lining fabric does not shrink when washed. The instructions given here are for making loose-lined curtains.

YOU WILL NEED

Fabric

Lining fabric

Weights (optional)

Thread

Headed tape

Hooks

Tools of the trade

Right Lined curtains hang well and add a fine finishing touch to the simplest of settings.

WHAT TO DO

1 Follow the measuring up and fabric calculation instructions on page 73.

2 Cut the curtain fabric and lining to the right sizes, making the lining 22.5cm (9in) shorter than the main fabric.

3 Join widths of fabric where required with a flat seam (see page 74) with a 12mm ($\frac{1}{2}$in) allowance. Cut notches along the selvedges at 15cm (6in) intervals. Press seams open.

4 Join pieces of lining in the same way. Lay lining on top of curtain with right sides together so that the top of the lining fabric is 7.5cm (3in) below the top of the main fabric and the side edges are matching.

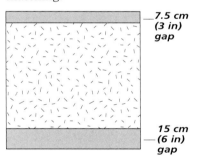

7.5 cm (3 in) gap

15 cm (6 in) gap

5 Pin and tack each side together and machine stitch 12mm ($\frac{1}{2}$in) from the edge, from the top to 15cm (6in) from the bottom. Make notches in the seam allowances. Turn right sides out. Press seam on each side so that there is approximately 2.5cm (1in) of fabric to the back of the curtain.

6 Turn up and press 5cm (2in) to the wrong side along the lower edge of the lining and make a double 2.5cm (1in) hem. Machine stitch.

7 Turn up and press 15cm (6in) to the wrong side of the main fabric along the lower edge, press in a mitre at each corner (see page 74) and tack a double 7.5cm (3in) hem, making the lining 5cm (2in) shorter than the curtain. To weight curtains, pop weights into the hem before stitching the mitres and bottom hem.

8 Turn down and press 7.5cm (3in) along the top of the curtain. Tack in place over the lining. Pin and tack the headed tape in place and complete as from step 9 on page 46.

BRIGHT IDEAS

❖ Make loops in a contrasting fabric, perhaps to match the lining.

❖ Personalize ready-made curtains with tiebacks.

❖ Add braid and cording to curtains for an individual finish.

❖ Use calico, silk or cheesecloth for lining your curtains.

❖ For more interesting linings, use contrasting fabric.

❖ Look for inspiration in books, paintings and old houses.

❖ Dispense with the rings supplied with a pole and use metallic clips instead.

❖ Personalize a plain wooden pole with paint to match or contrast with the curtain fabric. A verdigris effect, for example, would look very attractive.

MAKING HARD PELMETS

Hard pelmets are made from a rigid material such as wood, either painted or covered with fabric. Expensive to buy made-to-measure, they are, however, relatively easy to make. You simply need to fix a pelmet shelf to the window and you can then either add a wooden front and sides or cover the shelf with fabric.

To give the pelmet board some body and substance, cover it with interlining buckram or a self-adhesive stiffener before decorating it. Buckram is the traditional material to use. It is an open weave fabric that has been treated with fabric stiffener, and iron-on buckram is also available. It gives a very professional finish but requires quite a lot of fiddly hand sewing and needs to be backed with bump, interlining or iron-on interlining.

Self-adhesive stiffeners such as pelform are an easier choice. They come double or single sided: single-sided adhesive stiffener has a plush fabric on the reverse which means you don't need to back the fabric with lining.

BRIGHT IDEAS

❖ Enliven existing curtains with a pelmet made from an off-cut of fabric. Use either the same fabric or something that contrasts subtly or dramatically.

❖ Decorate a fabric-covered pelmet with starfish, shells, raffia, fake jewels - in fact, with anything that takes your fancy.

❖ Stiffen motifs from favourite fabrics (roses, teddies, whatever), and cut out and stick on to fabric pelmet.

YOU WILL NEED

Pelmet board (12mm [¹/₂in]
plywood, hardboard or
solid wood, cut to width of
window)
Small shelf-angled brackets
Graph paper

Self-adhesive stiffener
Pelmet fabric
Glue, velcro, staples or
tacks
Trimmings (as required)
Tools of the trade

WHAT TO DO

1 Position the pelmet board centrally over the window and just above the curtain track at the height you want the finished pelmet to come. Fix it in place with the brackets evenly spaced along the length of the board. This part is rather like putting up a shelf. Allow a clearance of about 2.5cm (1in) at each end of the track.

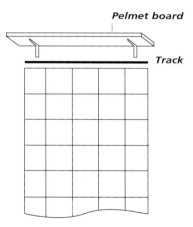

2 Measure along the front and around the sides of the pelmet board to give you the finished length of your pelmet.

3 Now draw the shape of the pelmet on to graph paper.

4 Transfer the design on to the self-adhesive stiffener and cut out.

5 Stick it on to the wrong side of your fabric, and trim the edges flush with the pelmet shape.

6 Stick on to the pelmet board with glue, velcro, staples or tacks. Where staples or tacks show, cover with braid.

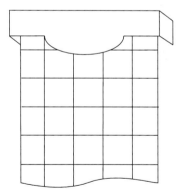

7 Decorate with trimmings as required.

Above A deep pelmet with contrasting piped edging helps balance the proportions of this window.

MAKING SIMPLE VALANCES AND SWAGS AND TAILS

Valances and swags and tails can give a formal and tailored finish to your window or, with a little bit of imagination, you can create a truly inspirational look for your room. Tailored valances and swags and tails can be complicated to make so follow our cheat's guide for lots of ideas that require little or no effort and skill.

WHAT TO DO

YOU WILL NEED

Valance track

Fabric

Thread

Swag hooks

Trimmings (as required)

Tools of the trade

1 For a valance, measure your valance track (including sides) and cut fabric according to the width required by your chosen headed tape (see pages 30-1) and making allowances for headings, hems and seams..

2 Make up as for unlined curtains (see pages 46-7).

3 For swags and tails, screw a swag hook into each side of the window above the track or pole and hang the fabric over the hooks in great swathes until you have achieved the effect you wish to create. Alternatively, make your own swag hooks - simply screw a wooden curtain ring into the pole through the eyelet and thread your fabric through the rings to create your swag.

4 Decorate the swag and tails with trimmings as required.

Left The traditional touch of matching floral curtains and valance gives a homely look to this landing.

Right A softly flowing valance is easy to make using lengths of net draped across and knotted around a wooden pole.

BRIGHT IDEAS

❖ Jazz up existing curtains with a valance made from an off-cut of fabric.

❖ Use a contrasting fabric in colour, pattern and also texture. A satin valance, for example, would look attractive in a bedroom.

❖ Add bows and rosettes to a simply draped swag to give a much grander and more tailored look.

❖ Add fringing and tassels to a swag and tail for an even more dramatic piece of window dressing.

MAKING TIEBACKS

Basic tiebacks are very straightforward to make and they are a simple way to finish off your curtains. They are also essential for curtains hanging in front of french doors, preventing them from getting in the way and collecting dirt and grime form the garden

WHAT TO DO

For a basic tieback

Graph paper

Fabric

Interfacing (optional)

Thread

Curtain rings

Tieback hooks

Tools of the trade

For a plaited tieback

Strips of foam

Fabric

Thread

Brass rings

Tieback hooks

Tools of the trade

Making a basic tieback

1 Use a tape measure to measure around the girth of the curtain to give you the finished length of your tieback.

2 Make a paper pattern cutting a rectangle of graph paper slightly larger than the required length of tieback and about 20cm (8in) deep.

3 Fold in half widthwise and draw out the shape of the tieback, as you would see it from the front of the curtain. If you plan to add bows, rosettes or other trimmings a simple rectangle may be all that is required. Cut out and open the paper flat.

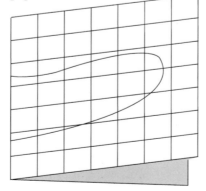

4 Using this pattern, cut out the fabric four times.

5 Cut out the interfacing if a formal look is required.

6 With right sides together, pin, tack and machine on three sides, leaving one short side open.

7 Turn right sides out and slip stitch the opening.

8 For difficult shapes, simply zigzag the fabric layers together on the right side.

Above *Scraps of fabric in a plaited tieback can help unite other colours and fabrics in your room scheme.*

Left
Tiebacks are a really neat way of keeping curtains away from windows.

9 Sew on curtain rings at each end to attach to tieback hooks on the wall.

Making a plaited tieback

1 Plait strips of foam into the lengths you require.

2 Separate the three lengths of foam.

3 Cut a strip of fabric to fit each length.

4 Wrap the fabric around each sausage of foam. Pin and tack. Remove foam and sew. Turn fabric to right side and re-thread foam.

5 Re-plait with the seam to the back and then finish each end neatly with a brass ring to attach to the tieback hooks on the wall.

MAKING ROSETTES AND BOWS

Rosettes and bows can be bought ready-made or in kits. But by following the simple instructions below you will find they are very easy to make. If you don't want to make a bow from two pieces of fabric as described below, tie a proper one from a long sash of fabric.

WHAT TO DO

Making a bow

1 Cut a piece of fabric twice the width of the finished bow plus 2.5cm (1in) for seam allowances and twice the depth of bow plus 2.5cm (1in) for seam allowances.

2 Fold the fabric in half lengthwise, with right sides together. Machine stitch along the long side, 12mm ($1/2$in) in from the edge.

3 Turn right sides out and press with seam to the centre of the fabric strip.

4 Fold into a double loop with the ends overlapping in the centre.

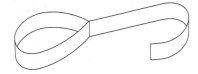

5 Run a line of vertical running stitches through the centre, draw up and secure. Stitch the 'bow' in place.

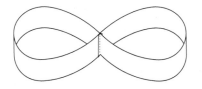

YOU WILL NEED

Fabric

Thread

Self-covering buttons (for rosettes)

Tools of the trade

. . . .

6 Cut a strip of fabric to cover the centre of the bow and form the knot. Turn in the side edges and wrap around the bow. Stitch in place.

7 If required, make a matching sash for the bow from a strip of fabric.

Making a rosette

1 Cut a strip of fabric 25 x 45cm (10 x 17in).

2 Fold it in half lengthwise with right sides together. Machine stitch 12mm ($1/2$in) from the length edge. Trim and press seam open.

3 Repeat with another piece of fabric. Turn the tubes right sides out and press the seam in the centre.

4 Place one strip over the other, with wrong sides facing up and join together as illustrated.

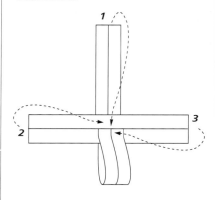

5 Secure with a contrasting covered button.

Above Bows can be used in many different ways. Here, they help to balance a matching fabric border.

BRIGHT IDEAS FOR OTHER TRIMMINGS

❖ Use cheerful ribbons to create 'bow' headings.

❖ Check out remnant sections in your soft furnishing departments. Trimmings can usually be picked up at bargain prices.

❖ Fringe your own fabrics (even weave only).

❖ Add a contrasting edging to curtains for a contemporary look.

BRIGHT IDEAS: CURTAINS

When making curtains you needn't restrict yourself to conventional techniques. Here are a few ideas for some more unusual ways of making and hanging curtains.

Below *Where a window covers a wall or where a curtain would encroach on a nearby doorway a single curtain is the answer.*

Above Customize a plain pair of calico curtains with cheerful checked edgings and matching loop headings. An iron pole completes the contemporary country look.

Left Add a real festive feel to your home with this instant curtain. A length of red silk fabric is draped and fixed with staples to a pelmet board. Add any number of decorations for instant appeal.

MAKING ROLLER BLINDS

Of all the different types of blinds that are available, roller blinds are by far the most straightforward to make and the finish they give to a window is both simple and smart. Many DIY kits are available too which make the job very easy.

WHAT TO DO

BRIGHT IDEAS

❖ Stencil or paint a design on to a plain fabric.

❖ Cut shapes out of the stiffened fabric blind.

❖ If using an even weave fabric, fringe the bottom of the blind.

1 Screw the brackets to the window. The slotted bracket which takes the spring should go on the left and the bracket for the end cap on the right.

2 Cut the roller to size, allowing about 3mm ($^1/_8$in) for the end cap and fit the end cap in place.

3 Stiffen the fabric following the instructions on the bottle carefully and allow to dry.

4 Cut the fabric to the width of the roller, minus 1cm ($^3/_8$in) and to the depth of the window plus 20cm (8in) for the heading and bottom casing. (Allow extra for any decorative edging you may wish to use.) Use a set square to ensure the fabric is cut at right angles.

5 The fabric shouldn't fray once the stiffener is painted on. If it does, however, zigzag the hem edges.

6 For a basic straight-edged blind, turn up a bottom hem to encase the batten and machine stitch in place.

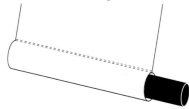

7 For a decorative edging, make a tuck to carry the batten allowing fabric to hang beneath it for the edging. Cut to the desired shape and zigzag stitch or bind the edge.

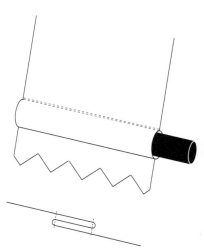

8 Attach the cord and cord holder to the centre back of the casing and batten.

9 Attach the fabric to the roller ensuring that it is straight according to the guidelines on the roller and glue, staple or tack in place.

10 Roll up the blind and slot it into the brackets. Attach the cord pull or acorn to the end of the cord.

Right *Bright florals used to good effect on a neat roller blind.*

MAKING ROMAN BLINDS

Roman blinds are very smart and they are economical to make
(a number of kits are available). They can be teamed with curtains
and pelmet for a traditional look or used on their own
for a modern look.
The folds in roman blinds are made by horizontal stitching
or casings slotted with dowels with rows of small curtain rings
stitched in place. A simpler method is to use roman blind tape which
has loops already attached. To make it easier to sew the horizontal
channels straight, use a fabric which has a horizontal line you can
follow. A check or horizontal stripe would be ideal.

WHAT TO DO

YOU WILL NEED

Fabric

Lining

Lath 2.5cm (1in) wide

Wooden dowels 12mm (1/2in)
diameter and cut to finished
width of blind less 5cm (2in)

Thread

Small curtain rings

Cleat and screws

Nylon cord (lots!)

Batten 5 x 2.5cm (2 x 1in) cut
to finished width of blind

Staples or tacks

Screw eyes

Wooden acorn

Tools of the trade

1 Cut the main fabric of the blind to the finished size plus 6cm ($2^{1}/_{2}$in) for side turnings and 19cm ($7^{1}/_{2}$in) for the lower edge. Also allow 5cm (2in) for fixing the fabric to the batten.

2 Cut the lining to the same size as the finished blind plus 5cm (2in) at top.

3 Join fabric widths where necessary with a flat seam (see page 74).

4 Lay the lining on top of the main fabric with right sides facing. Position the lining so that the top edges are level and the lower edge is 19cm ($7^{1}/_{2}$in) shorter than main fabric.

5 Stitch the side seams with 1.5cm ($5/_{8}$in) seam allowance. Press seams open.

6 Turn right sides out and press so the lining is centred on the main fabric.

7 Make a casing at the base of the blind by turning up 12mm ($1/_{2}$in) and then a further 18cm (7in). Stitch. This casing will carry the lath.

8 Mark the positions for the casings that will carry the dowels - they should be approximately 30cm (12in) apart. The distance between the casings should not be more than twice the distance from the lowest casing to the lower edge of the blind. The distance from the top casing to the batten should be the same as the spacing between all the other casings. Stitch the casings with two rows of stitches 1.5cm ($5/_{8}$in) apart.

9 Unpick a couple of stitches in one of the side seams each time it crosses a casing. Insert a dowel and re-stitch the seam neatly.

10 Stitch rings in rows down each side and one or more rows in the middle - ensure that the rings align across the blind.

11 Position the cleat on the wall next to the blind.

12 Cut the cord into appropriate lengths; one to run up the blind, across the top and down the other side, and another to run up the blind, and hang down the same side again. Cut further lengths of cord for any additional rows of rings and allow lots of extra cord for knotting and operating the blind.

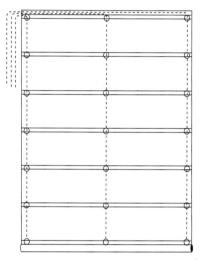

13 Tie one end of each cord to the bottom ring on each side of the blind.

14 cover the batten with matching fabric if desired and fix to the wall or window frame.

15 Staple or tack the top of the blind to the batten using the 5cm (2in) fabric allowance made. Make sure the blind is straight.

16 Mark the positions of the rows of rings on the batten and screw in eyes to correspond.

17 Thread the cords through the screw eyes and pass over to the cleat side of the blind.

Above Roman blinds fit into just about any setting including this neo-classical one. Always a good choice where you want to show off a beautiful print.

18 Knot the ends of the cord and cover with a wooden acorn.

BRIGHT IDEAS

❖ Add a decorative border and a matching pelmet.

❖ Add a paint effect to plain fabric before making up.

❖ Use a semi-sheer fabric such as open weave linen or cotton for a crisp look.

MAKING AUSTRIAN BLINDS

Austrian blinds work on the same principle as roman blinds except that they have a gathered or pleated heading and no wooden dowels. When drawn up they fall into soft swags, usually ending with a ruffle. Austrian blind tape is used in place of the wooden dowels and this is available either ready for use with loops or just with pockets into which rings are inserted.

WHAT TO DO

YOU WILL NEED

Fabric

Thread

Austrian blind tape

Heading tape

Curtain hooks

Curtain track

Rings (optional)

Wooden batten, cut to width of window

Brass screw eyes

Cleat and screws

Nylon cord

Wooden acorn

Tools of the trade

1 Measure the window from track to sill and add 45cm (18in). Multiply by the width dictated by the heading tape (normally twice - see pages 30-1)

2 Join the widths of fabric where necessary with a flat open seam (see page 74).

3 Hem the bottom and sides of the fabric or attach a matching frill.

4 Sew vertical lines of austrian blind tape down either edge of the wrong side of the blind and at intervals of approximately 60cm (24in). If you are using tape with loops, ensure they align horizontally when stitching on the second line. If you are using the other kind of tape align the pockets in the same way and then slot the rings in place. Start at the bottom left-hand corner and slot a ring through a pocket on the first length of tape, 5cm (2in) up from the bottom edge of the blind. Attach rings 20cm (8in) apart. Repeat for other tapes again making sure the rings - like the pockets - align horizontally.

5 Turn down and press a 3mm ($^{1}/_{8}$in) hem at the top of the blind. Sew on the heading tape, following the instructions on page 46 for fixing heading tape. Position the curtain hooks.

6 Draw up the cord of the heading tape to fit the window, knot the cords and wind around a curtain hook.

7 Mount the track on to the batten and then the batten to the window.

8 Screw in the brass screw eyes, positioning them on the underside of the batten and in line with each vertical tape.

9 Mount the cleat on the wall beside the blind.

10 Starting at the opposite end of the blind to the cleat, knot a length of the cord to the bottom loop. Then thread the cord through all the loops or rings on the vertical tape.

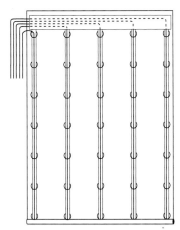

Above Clean, fresh, and very elegant, austrian blinds look just as at home in the breakfast room as bedroom.

11 Thread it through the screw eyes along the batten and down to the cleat. Wrap around the cleat several times.

12 Repeat this process with each vertical tape.

13 Cover the ends of the cord with the wooden acorn for a neat finish.

MAKING FESTOON BLINDS

Make the most of a simple window with an elegant festoon blind. They make the perfect choice for a bathroom or bedroom where luxury and comfort are required.

YOU WILL NEED

Fabric

Thread

Heading tape

Curtain hooks

Curtain track

Festoon blind tape

Wooden batten

Brass screw eyes

Cleat and screws

Festoon blind cord

Wooden acorn

Festoon blind rings

Right Always a good choice for a pretty bathroom, festoon blinds exude a sense of luxury.

WHAT TO DO

1 Measure the window from track to sill and multiply by 1¹/₂ to 2 times then multiply the finished width by two.

2 Join widths of fabric where necessary with a flat open seam (see page 74).

3 Hem the bottom and both sides of the fabric, or attach a frill if required.

4 Turn and press 3mm (¹/₈in) hem at the top of the blind. Sew on heading tape as for an austrian blind (see previous page).

5 Sew festoon blind tape at each edge of the fabric 2.5cm (1in) in from the edge and at 45cm (18in) intervals using just one row of stitches down the centre of the tape.

6 Knot the vertical draw cords at the base of the tape.

7 Draw up the cords of the heading tape to fit the width of the window, and wrap around a curtain hook as before (see austrian blind on previous page).

8 Draw up each of the vertical cords from the top of the blind to give the desired drop. Do not cut off the cords but tie them neatly at the top of each tape.

9 Fix a batten to the top of the window and insert brass screw eyes, positioning them on the underside of the batten and in line with each vertical tape.

10 Mount the track to the face of the batten.

11 Position and secure the brass cleat.

12 Insert the bottom loop of each vertical tape through one of the festoon blind rings and then pull the loop around the outer rim of the ring to fasten it securely.

13 Starting at the opposite end of the blind to the cleat, thread the cord through every other loop on the first vertical tape, first knotting the cord around the bottom festoon blind ring. Then thread through the screw eyes leaving enough cord hanging to wrap around the cleat and operate the blind. Repeat for each vertical tape.

14 Finish the ends of the blind cord neatly with the wooden acorn.

BRIGHT IDEAS

❖ Use a sheer fabric and sew on sequins, tiny shells, seeds or beads for a contemporary look.

❖ A cheap and cheerful gingham would look good in a nursery.

Above Decorative braid edgings and cord detail heading make these roman blinds unique.

Right A width of fabric is simply hung at a window and tied up into ruches. Temporary effect decorations in the form of fairy lights and unconventional hardware in the form of branches help complete the festive scene. For a more conventional look, experiment with muslin hung on a length of net wire and add satin ribbon ties.

BRIGHT IDEAS: BLINDS

Here are three unusual ways to use blinds, ranging from something that is quite straightforward to make (left) to a more complicated arangement (opposite, bottom). Trimmings are very useful for making your window dressings that little bit different, and by using fabrics that are uncommonly used for blinds, such as tea towels or a delicate sheer fabric, you can create something that is unique.

Left *A simple tie blind is effective and very easy to make. The blind is hung simply from a batten. A dowel is sewn into the bottom hem and the blind is simply rolled up and tied with matching ties.*

BASICS

Before you start to make your own window dressings it is important to familiarize yourself with the tools of the trade and the basic techniques.

Here we set out to introduce you to what you need for the job, show you how to measure up, how to choose fabric, describe simple sewing techniques and provide a glossary of fabrics and a list of addresses where you will find all the materials and tools mentioned in this book.

You may not wish to invest in all the tools initially. Perhaps you could start by borrowing from friends and relations and gradually build up your stock and skills as you go along.

Accuracy really is the key to good window dressing skills so follow our suggestions and check all measurements and calculations carefully.

If you are starting from scratch, practise the simple sewing techniques on off-cuts of fabrics before you begin your project. This will help build up your confidence and practice really does make perfect!

Lastly, hopefully the glossary of fabrics will give you inspiration to experiment and our list of addresses will be sure to offer yet more inspiring ideas.

Right *Nothing beats the satisfaction of making something well, so make sure you are well organized and prepared before you start the job.*

BEFORE YOU START

Having all the correct tools of the trade will make the job much easier and the finished result better. These are listed below.

CUTTING FABRIC

To get a good professional finish lay the fabric out on a number of tables joined together or invest in a large trestle table. If you don't have a suitable table then use the floor, but the results will not be as good. Pin out and mark your fabric and be very sure you have your measurements right before you cut out the fabric. Mistakes are commonly made with patterned fabrics, so take lots of time to match the pattern when joining widths. Fabrics with a sheer or pile, like satin and velvet, need to be treated in the same way as patterned fabrics and laid so the different widths have the pile lying in the same direction.

PROFESSIONAL TIPS

❖ Use sharp, good quality scissors.
❖ Invest in the best quality scissors you can afford, they will really make the job much easier.
❖ Pinking sheers prevent fine fabrics from fraying and cut down on oversewing.
❖ Curtain maker's clamps help keep fabric in position when cutting and sewing, and are particularly useful when you have very heavy curtains to make.
❖ Cut fabric on a table if possible and not on the floor.
❖ A trestle table will be a worthwhile investment. No professional curtain maker would attempt to make curtains on the floor.

WHAT YOU NEED

Sewing machine

Iron

Good quality dressmaking scissors

Needlework scissors for trimming

Pinking sheers

Large table if possible

Curtain maker's clamps

Good quality metal tape measure

Plastic ruler

Pins and needles

Tailor's chalk

Step ladder

MEASURING UP

Measuring up accurately is most important to avoid expensive mistakes. Use a good quality metal measure and check your measurements several times.

TO MEASURE UP

1 Have the curtain rod or track in place before taking any measurements.

2 Measure from the top of the curtain track, or if using a pole or rod, from the point at which the top of the curtain will hang to the desired length of the curtain (the finished length). Add 22cm (8½in) for hems and headings.

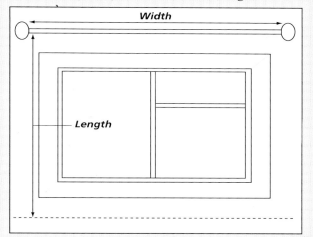

3 Next measure the width of the track or pole and add 5cm (2in) for each side hem and 15cm (6in) if the curtains are to overlap.

TO CALCULATE FABRIC QUANTITIES

1 Multiply the finished width by the gathering width of the heading tape to be used.

2 Divide by the width of the fabric and round up to the nearest figure. Then you can calculate the number of widths you require.

3 Multiply the number of fabric widths by the measured length in order to calculate the amount of fabric required.

4 If the fabric chosen has a pattern repeat, allow one depth of pattern repeat for each width.

SIMPLE SEWING TECHNIQUES

STITCHES

Slip stitch This stitch is useful for holding hems in place nearly invisibly. Make a tiny stitch in the main fabric, picking up one or two threads, close to the folded edge opposite the first stitch. Then bring it out 6mm ($1/4$in) to the left and pull through.

Running stitch This stitch is used to aid gathering in fabrics. Work small, even, running stitches in two rows a short distance apart. Gather fabric to the desired amount and fasten off any loose ends.

Tacking Temporary 1cm ($1/2$in) long running stitches used to hold fabric in position.

MAKING BASIC FLAT SEAMS

Use this seam for joining widths of fabric.

1 Place the two pieces of fabric to be joined right sides together, with raw edges aligned.

2 Pin and tack just inside the seam line. Sew 1.5cm ($5/8$in) in from the raw edges, working a few stitches in reverse at each end to secure the threads.

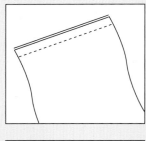

3 Remove tacking and press the seam open.

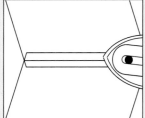

MITRING CORNERS

1 Turn in the sides of the curtain and then the hem and press.

2 Open out fabric again and turn the corner edge in to the centre following pressing lines.

3 Turn in the side turnings.

4 Finally, turn up the hem to form the mitre and slip stitch in place.

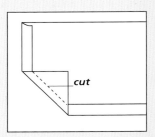

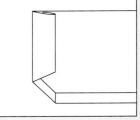

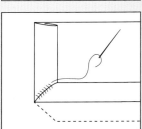

MAKING SINGLE FRILLS

1 Add 1.5cm ($5/8$in) seam allowance to the desired finished depth and an allowance of 1-2cm ($3/8$-$3/4$in) for a double hem.

2 The overall length should be $1^1/2$ times the required finished length plus seam allowances. Join the strips where necessary with a flat seam (see left).

3 Allow 12mm ($1/2$in) at each end to make a 6mm ($1/4$in) double hem if required.

4 To finish, turn under the double hem along the bottom edge and ends.

5 Divide the length into equal sections and run two rows of running stitches along the raw edge within these sections.

6 Pin the frill to the main fabric, tack and sew into place.

CHOOSING FABRIC

When choosing your fabric visit as many soft furnishing departments as possible and ask for advice. If you don't find the fabric you are looking for, do not despair, you can usually track it down through mail order. Collect together pieces of fabric that you like. Small scraps of fabric are really of no use. You really need a large piece of fabric - at least half a metre (yard) - to give you a good idea of what the fabric would look like made up. Try draping the fabric over your track or pole at the window in question to see the different effects you can achieve with the fabric. Softly draped voile would soften a harsh modern window, for example, and a crisp striped cotton would make a bold statement as a roman blind.

Bear in mind that certain fabrics are better suited to some treatments than others. Chintz and voile will drape well, while heavier fabrics like velvet and brocade will hang in more formal folds.

Always try the fabric out at home. You are in danger of making an expensive mistake if you buy fabric under the glare of fluorescent shop light. If you happen on a "too good to miss" bargain sale and want to buy fabric on spec, at least take the fabric into natural light before making a decision.

Above Choosing your fabric can be a difficult decision - do you want something to tone with the rest of the room's decor, or do you go for something that contrasts?

PRACTICAL POINTERS

❖ Fabric should drape well.

❖ Will you need to match a difficult pattern?

❖ Is fabric washable or will you need to get it dry cleaned?

Bright ideas

❖ Use cheaper fabrics like ticking, calico and muslin.

❖ Try using unusual fabrics like sail cloth, parachute silk and cheesecloth.

FABRIC GLOSSARY

Fabrics

Brocade Fine fabric patterned with raised floral motifs, usually made from silk.

Butter muslin Very economical loose-weave fabric which is almost translucent. It is ideal for making softly swathing drapes and swags.

Calico Firm, plain cotton.

Chintz Made from cotton finished with a shiny glaze that is easily lost if care is not taken. Available in all manner of colours and patterns, but most traditionally in bright florals.

Crewelwork Indian cotton fabric, decorated with hand sewn embroidery in elaborate colours and patterns of chain stitch.

Damask Cotton or silk woven with large patterns of leaves and flowers giving contrast in texture between matt and satin threads.

Gingham A checked cotton fabric which fits equally well into modern or traditional settings.

Lace Openwork fabric usually made of cotton.

Madras cotton Brightly coloured fabric with a checked or striped design from India.

Moiré A watermark effect on silk. Effective for grand drapes.

Satin Fabric with sheen on one side.

Ticking A striped cotton fabric originally used in a utilitarian way to cover mattresses. Very cheap and fits well into all settings.

Velvet A cotton fabric with a pile which gives a soft surface.

Voile Translucent fabric ideal for draping.

Linings

Blackout Opaque material which totally excludes the light.

Interlining Dense soft cotton fabric used between fabric and lining.

Buckram An open weave fabric impregnated with adhesive and stiffened. Used as the base for hard pelmets.

Bump Blanket-like interlining which is sewn into a curtain or pelmet between the fabric and the lining. Has good thermal qualities and gives a full look.

Cotton sateen The usual lining for curtains and blinds and comes in a variety of weights and widths.

Interfacing Iron-on stiffening fabric for tiebacks.

Millium (aluminium coated thermal) Used to give greater insulation to curtains and blinds.

STOCKISTS AND SUPPLIERS

Fabrics

Laura Ashley
256-8 Regent Street
Oxford Circus
London W1R 5DA
(traditional selection)

Jane Churchill
135 Sloane Street
London SW1X 9LP
(traditional selection)

The Conran Shop
81 Fulham Road
London SW3 6RD
(contemporary fabrics)

Thomas Dare
341 King's Road
London SW3 5ES
(contemporary fabrics)

Designer's Guild
277 King's Road
London SW3 5EN
(modern classics)

Habitat
19-20 Kings Mall
King Street
London W6 0QS
(contemporary fabrics)

Ikea
Drury Way
North Circular Road
London NW10 0JQ
(budget fabrics)

John Lewis
278-306 Oxford Street
London W1R 6AH
(everything under one roof)

Knickerbean
Holywell Hill
St Albans
Herts
(cut price fabrics)

Liberty
210-20 Regent Street
London W1R 6AH
(wide range of fabrics and
sewing materials)

Ian Mankin
109 Regent's Park Road
London NW1 8UR
(contemporary fabrics in
stripes, checks and natural
materials)

Nice Irma's
46 Goodge Street
London W1P 1F
(Indian fabrics)

Nursery Window
83 Walton Street
London SW3 2HP
(wide range of fabrics for
children's rooms)

Russell and Chapple
23 Monmouth Street
London WC2 9DE
(cheap and cheerful range of
calico and other natural fabrics)

Trimmings

VV Rouleaux
201 New King's Road
London SW6 4SR

Distinctive Trimmings
17 A Kensington Church
Street
London W8 4LF

Hardware

Artisan
797 Wandsworth Road
London SW8 3JT
(metal forged hardware)

Merchants
Olmar Wharf
Olmar Street
London SE1 5AY
(metal forged hardware)

Byron & Byron
4 Hanover Yard
London N1 8BE
(imaginative rods, poles and
holdbacks)

Hang Ups Accessories Ltd
7 Lyncroft Farm Workshops
Perrott's Brook
Cirencester
Gloucestershire
GL7 7BW

McKinney Kidston
1 Wandon Road
London SW6 2JF
(clip-on curtain rings)

Silent Glis
Star Lane
Margate
Kent
(high quality tracks)

Harrison Drape
Bradford Street
Birmingham
B12 0PE
(tracks and accessories)

Jali Ltd
Apsley House
Chartham
Canterbury
Kent CT4 7HT
(wooden pelmets)

Blinds

Sunway
Mersey Industrial Estate
Heaton Mersey
Stockport
Cheshire SK4 3EQ
(wide range of quality blinds)

Appeal Blinds
Unit 16
Barnack Industrial Estate
Novers Hill
Bedminster
Bristol BS3 5QE
(conservatory blinds)

Making up

Rufflette
Sharston Road
Wythenshawe
Manchester
M22 4TH
(everything for curtain mak-
ing)

Morplan
56 Great Titchfield Street
London W1P 8DX
(curtain makers' clamps)

INDEX

The page numbers in *italics* represent illustrations

ACKNOWLEDGMENTS

The author and publisher would like to thank the following companies and people for their help with supplying photographs for this book:

Front cover: HB/Trevor Richards (main), HB/Spike Powell, Rufflette, Artisan, HB/David Burgess

Back cover: The Shutter Shop

Page 3, Harrison Drape; pages 4-5, Sunway Blinds; page 6, Sunway Blinds; pages 8-9, Sunway Blinds; page 10, HB/Derek Lomas; page 11, HB/Ian Sanderson; page 12, Sunway Blinds; page 13, HB/Trevor Richards; page 14, HB/Spike Powell; page 15, HB/Steve Hawkins; page 16, HB/Trevor Richards; page 18, HB/Spike Powell; page 19, Harrison Drape; page 20, HB/Steve Hawkins; page 21, Appeal Blinds; pages 22-3, HB/Spike Powell; page 24, Sunway Blinds; page 25, HB/Roy Smith; page 26, Swish; page 27, Crown; page 28, HB/Ron Kelly; pages 32-3, HB/Chris Bayley; page 35, Artisan; page 36, Jali Ltd; page 37, HB/Trevor Richards; page 38, HB/Derek Lomas; pages 38-9, Wendy Cushing Trimmings Ltd; page 40, Sunway Blinds; page 41, HB/David Burgess; page 42, Faber PR; page 43, The Shutter Shop; page 45, Sanderson; pages 46-7, Harrison Drape; pages 48-9, Swish; pages 50-1, Sanderson; page 52, Harrison Drape; page 53, HB/Ian Kalinowski; pages 54-5, Rufflette; page 55, HB/Derek Lomas; page 57, Harrison Drape; page 58, HB/Ian Kalinowski; pages 58-9, HB/Trevor Richards; page 59, HB/Trevor Richards; page 61, Harrison Drape; page 63, Sanderson; page 65, Sunway Blinds; pages 66-7, HB/Ian Sanderson; page 68 top, HB/Spike Powell; page 68 bottom, HB/Trevor Richards; page 69, Sanderson; pages 70-1, Harrison Drape; page 75, Sanderson.

THOUGHTS & QUOTATIONS
BY WOMEN
ABOUT MOTHERHOOD

I Am Mother

A Chinese writer,
Lin Yutang, wrote:
'Of all the rights of women,
the greatest is to be a mother.'

ALicat

Alicat Publishing
16 Sandilands Street
South Melbourne VIC 3205
Australia
Email: publishing@alicat.com.au
www.alicat.com.au

Publisher: Ali Horgan
Project Manager: Angie McKenzie
Design: Canary Graphic Design

First published 2012
Printed in China 5 4 3 2 1
AC11 166

Preface

Of all the jobs in the world, motherhood or being a mother is undoubtedly one of the most important. Without a mother, the institution of family would not have begun. Mothers are the rock that all families revolve around and the backbone of their very being.

A mother, mum, mom, momma or mama, is defined as a woman who has raised a child, to whom she may or may not have given birth, in the role of parent.

Because of the complexity and differences of a mother's social, cultural and religious definitions and roles, it is challenging to define a mother to suit a universally accepted definition. Challenging that is – but not impossible.

For such a pivotal role, strangely there is no training for motherhood. Because of this, mothers are not always perfect, sometimes far from it. They can miss the mark and spend many hours a day worrying and fretting about their choices and decisions.

The thing that sets a mother's role in the family apart from everyone else is her everlasting love for her children and her intent that they lead normal, well-adjusted lives. She puts ahead of anything else, the rights and needs of her child and will work and fight tirelessly towards the best possible result for them.

Her role is widespread from nurturer, to doctor, nurse, housekeeper, cook, driver, personal secretary, teacher, sporting coach, counsellor, consoler and best friend.

Motherhood is a life sentence. There is no end to the role, no time when it's up. Once a mother, she will stay a mother for the whole of her life. This role will be filled with a mixture of laughter, tears, stress and promise.

It will be her greatest joy, her deepest sadness, her biggest frustration and her most celebrated accomplishment.

No one will love you like your mother!

Making the decision to have a child is momentous.
It is to decide forever to have your heart
go walking around outside your body.

ELIZABETH STONE

Mother is the one we count on
for the things
that matter most of all.

KATHARINE BUTLER HATHAWAY
American author (1890–1942)

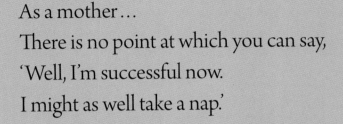

As a mother…
There is no point at which you can say,
'Well, I'm successful now.
I might as well take a nap.'

CARRIE FISHER
American actress and author (1956–)

She never quite leaves her children at home,
even when she doesn't take them along.

MARGARET CULKIN BANNING
American author (1891–1982)

The best conversations with mothers
always take place in silence,
when only the heart speaks.

CARRIE LATET

Motherhood cannot finally be delegated.
Breast-feeding may succumb to the bottle;
cuddling, fondling, and paediatric visits may
also be done by fathers ...
but when a child needs a mother to talk to,
nobody else but a mother will do.

ERICA JONG
American author and teacher (1942–)

Biology is the least
of what makes someone a mother.

OPRAH WINFREY
American actress and producer (1954–)

When you are a mother,
you are never really alone in your thoughts.
A mother always has to think twice,
once for herself and once for her child.

SOPHIA LOREN
Italian actress (1934–)

Mother love is the fuel that enables
a normal human being to do the impossible.

MARION C. GARRETTY

Then someone placed her in my arms.
She looked up at me.
The crying stopped.
Her eyes melted through me,
forging a connection in me with their soft heat.

SHIRLEY MACLAINE
American actress and author (1934–)

Children and mothers never truly part –
Bound in the beating of each other's heart.

CHARLOTTE GRAY
Canadian historian and author (1948–)

Being a mother is learning about strengths
you didn't know you had,
and dealing with fears you didn't know existed.

LINDA WOOTEN

Now, as always,
the most automated appliance in a household
is the mother.

BEVERLY JONES

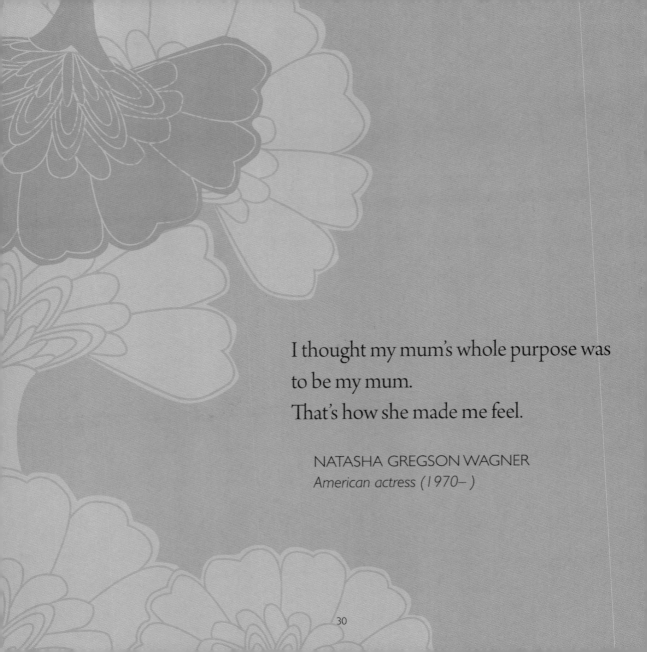

I thought my mum's whole purpose was
to be my mum.
That's how she made me feel.

NATASHA GREGSON WAGNER
American actress (1970–)

There is no way to be a perfect mother,
and a million ways to be a good one.

JILL CHURCHILL
American writer (1943–)

Of all the rights of women,
the greatest is to be a mother.

LIN YUTANG
Chinese writer and inventor (1895–1976)

Some mothers are kissing mothers
and some are scolding mothers,
but it is love just the same,
and most mothers kiss and scold together.

PEARL S. BUCK
American writer (1892–1973)

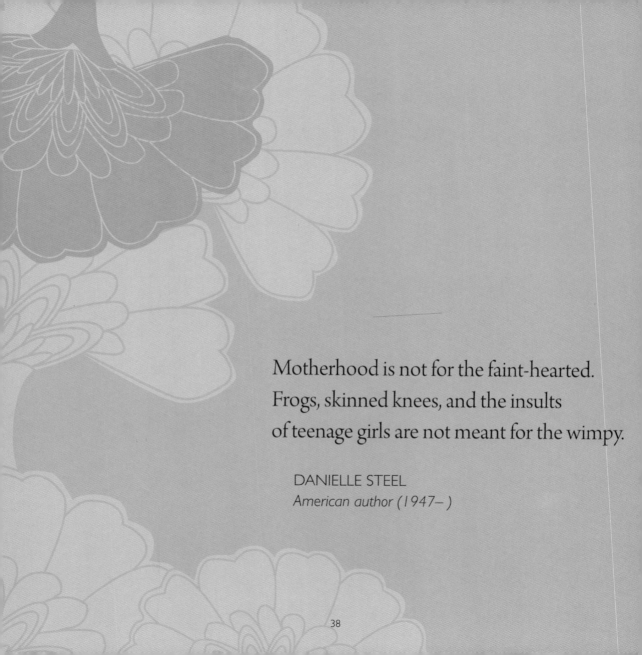

Motherhood is not for the faint-hearted.
Frogs, skinned knees, and the insults
of teenage girls are not meant for the wimpy.

DANIELLE STEEL
American author (1947–)

It was my mother who taught us
to stand up to our problems,
not only in the world around us
but in ourselves.

DOROTHY PITMAN HUGHES
American writer, speaker and activist

There is a point at which you aren't
as much mum and daughter
as you are adults and friends.

JAMIE LEE CURTIS
American actress and author (1958–)

Those who say they
'Sleep like a baby'
haven't got one.

A NEW MOTHER

I love being a mother … I am more aware.
I feel things on a deeper level.
I have a kind of understanding about my
body, about being a woman.

SHELLEY LONG
American actress (1949–)

It was my mother who gave me my voice.
She did this, I know now,
by clearing a space where my words could fall, grow,
then find their way to others.

PAULA GIDDINGS
African-American historian and writer (1947–)

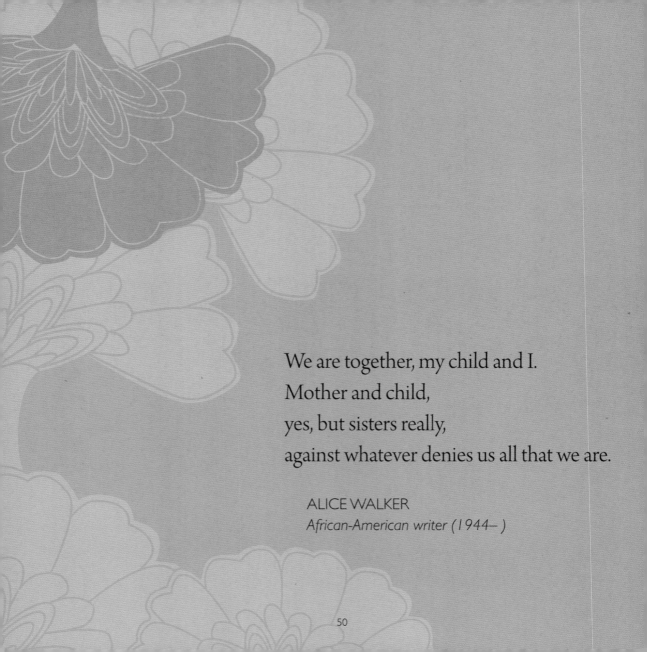

We are together, my child and I.
Mother and child,
yes, but sisters really,
against whatever denies us all that we are.

ALICE WALKER
African-American writer (1944–)

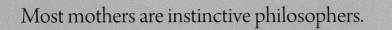

Most mothers are instinctive philosophers.

HARRIET BEECHER STOWE
American abolitionist and author (1811–1896)

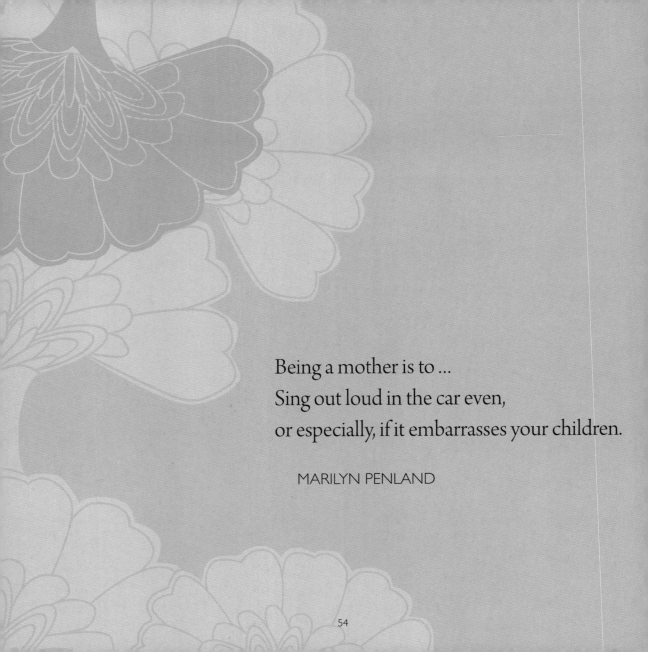

Being a mother is to ...
Sing out loud in the car even,
or especially, if it embarrasses your children.

MARILYN PENLAND

Before becoming a mother
I had a hundred theories on how
to bring up children.
Now I have seven children
and only one theory:
Love them,
especially when they least deserve to be loved.

KATE SAMPERI
Writer and columnist

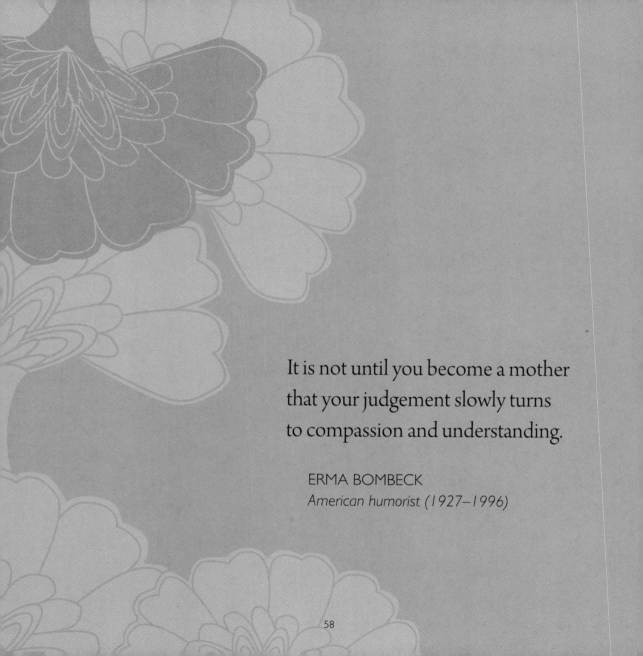

It is not until you become a mother that your judgement slowly turns to compassion and understanding.

ERMA BOMBECK
American humorist (1927–1996)

Only a mother knows a mother's fondness.

LADY MARY WORTLEY MONTAGU
English aristocrat and writer (1689–1762)

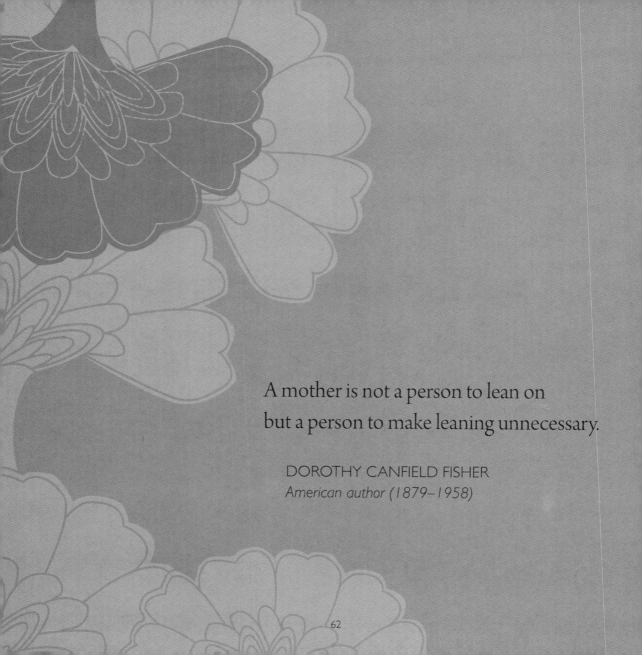

A mother is not a person to lean on
but a person to make leaning unnecessary.

DOROTHY CANFIELD FISHER
American author (1879–1958)

The story of a mother's life:
Trapped between a scream and a hug.

CATHY GUISEWITE
American cartoonist (1950–)

Motherhood is ...
Never being number one in your list
of priorities
and not minding at all.

JASMINE GUINNESS
Irish model and designer (1976–)

The older I become,
the more I think about my mother.

INGMAR BERGMAN
Swedish director, writer and producer (1918–2007)

As a parent you try to maintain a certain
amount of control
and so you have this tug-of-war ...
you have to learn when to let go.
And that's not easy.

ARETHA FRANKLIN
American singer (1942–)

Being a full-time mother
is one of the highest salaried jobs in my field
since the payment is pure love.

MILDRED B. VERMONT

On my mother ...
My love for her and my hate for her
are so bafflingly intertwined
that I can hardly see her.
I never know who is who.
She is me and I am she and we're all together.

ERICA JONG
American author (1942–)

A mother's love liberates.

MAYA ANGELOU
American author and poet (1928–)

One of the oldest human needs
is having someone to wonder
where you are when you don't come
home at night.

MARGARET MEAD
American cultural anthropologist (1901–1978)

Discovering that with every child,
your heart grows bigger and stronger –
that there is no limit to how much
or how many people you can love,
even though at times you feel
as though you could burst –
you don't –
you just love even more.

YASMIN LE BON
British-Iranian fashion model (1964–)

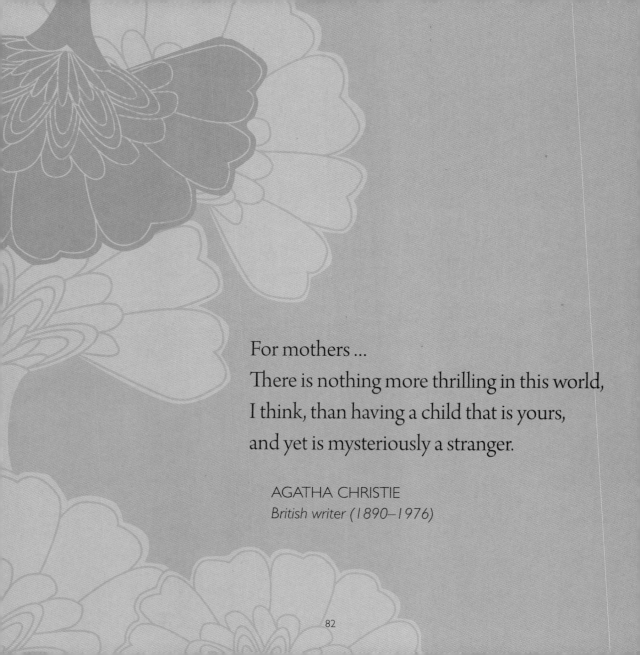

For mothers ...
There is nothing more thrilling in this world,
I think, than having a child that is yours,
and yet is mysteriously a stranger.

AGATHA CHRISTIE
British writer (1890–1976)

By and large, mothers and housewives
are the only workers
who do not have regular time off.
They are the great vacationless class.

ANNE MORROW LINDBERGH
American aviator and author (1906–2001)

A mother's advice …
The real menace in dealing with a
five-year-old is that in no time at all you
begin to sound
like a five-year-old.

JEAN KERR
American author (1922–2003)

I looked on child-rearing not only as
a work of love and duty
but as a profession that was
fully as interesting and challenging
as any honourable profession in the world
and one that demanded the best
that I could bring it.

ROSE KENNEDY
American author (1890–1995)

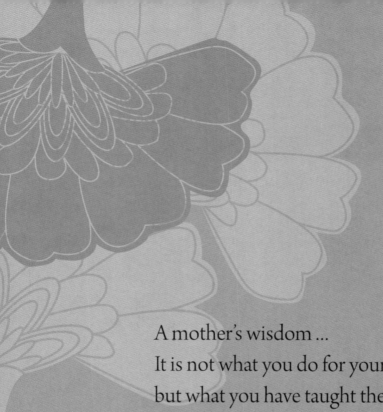

A mother's wisdom ...
It is not what you do for your children
but what you have taught them to do
for themselves
that will make them successful human beings.

ANN LANDERS
Pen name for Ruth Crowley, American author (1918–2002)

Our children are not going to be just 'our children' –
they are going to be other people's husbands and wives
and the parents of our grandchildren.

MARY S. CALDERONE
American physician (1904–1998)

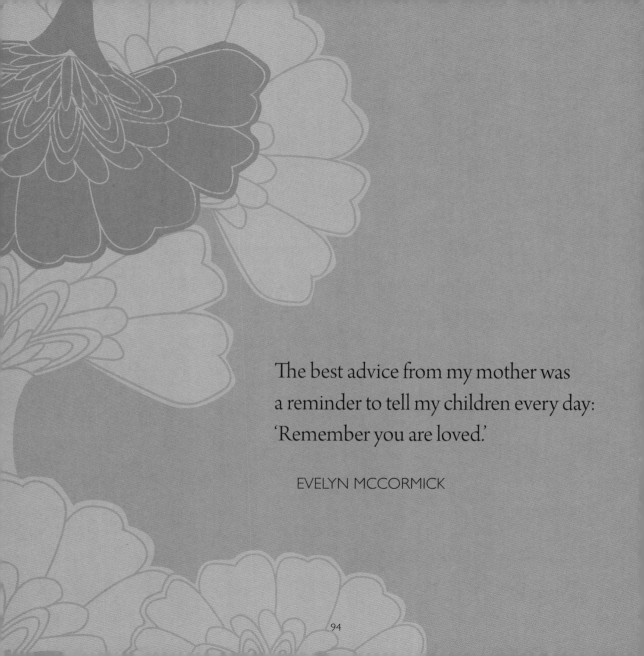

The best advice from my mother was
a reminder to tell my children every day:
'Remember you are loved.'

EVELYN MCCORMICK

My son is my son 'till he gets him a wife,
but my daughter's my daughter
all the days of her life.

AUTHOR UNKNOWN

Loving a child doesn't mean giving in
to all his whims;
to love him is to bring out the best in him,
to teach him to love what is difficult.

NADIA BOULANGER
French composer and teacher (1887–1979)

When I stopped seeing my mother
with the eyes of a child,
I saw the woman who
helped me give birth to myself.

NANCY FRIDAY
American author (1933–)

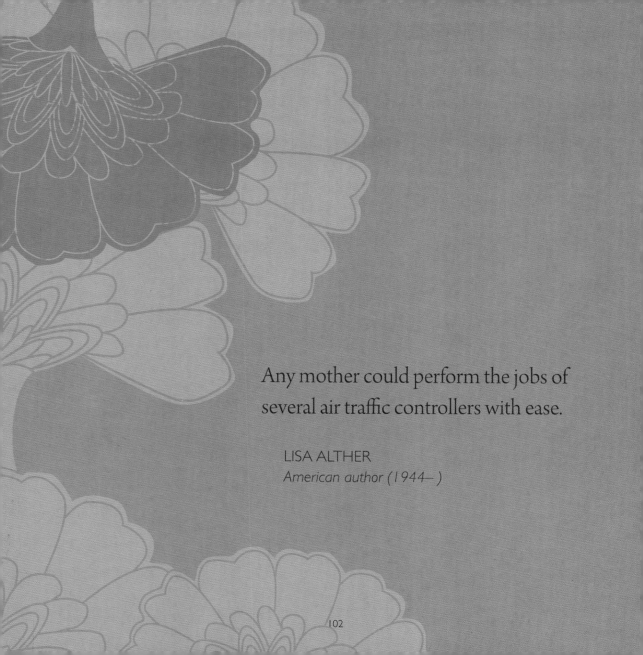

Any mother could perform the jobs of
several air traffic controllers with ease.

LISA ALTHER
American author (1944–)

A mother's arms are more comforting
than anyone else's.

DIANA, PRINCESS OF WALES
*Member of the British royal family
and humanitarian (1961–1997)*

No matter how old a mother is,
she watches her middle-aged children
for signs of improvement.

FLORIDA SCOTT-MAXWELL
Author, playwright and psychologist (1883–1979)

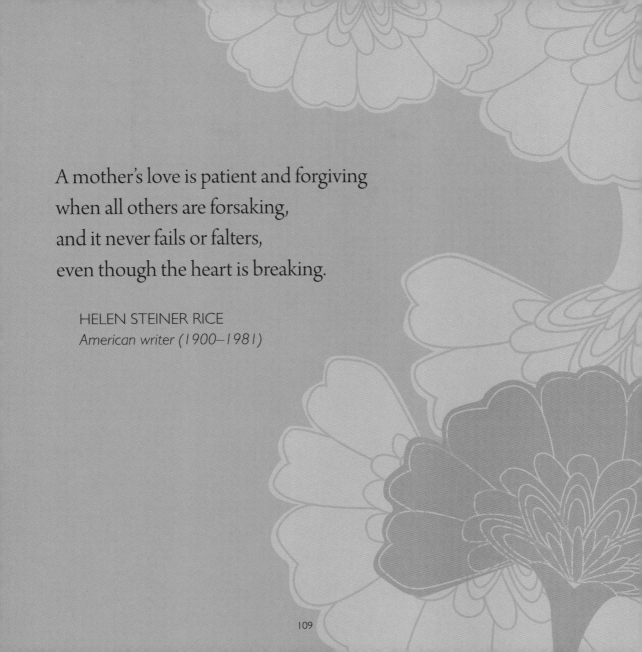

A mother's love is patient and forgiving
when all others are forsaking,
and it never fails or falters,
even though the heart is breaking.

HELEN STEINER RICE
American writer (1900–1981)

In the sheltered simplicity
of the first days after a baby is born,
one sees again the magical closed circle,
the miraculous sense of two people
existing only for each other.

ANNE MORROW LINDBERGH
American aviator and author (1906–2001)

My mother is my mirror and I am hers.
What do we see?
Our face grown young again.

MARGE PIERCY
American poet and author (1936–)

My mom is a never-ending song in my
heart of comfort, happiness, and being.
I may sometimes forget the words
but I always remember the tune.

GRAYCIE HARMON

It's not easy being a mother.
If it were easy,
fathers would do it.

THE GOLDEN GIRLS
American sitcom (1985–1992)

A mother's wish ...
A hundred years from now ...
it will not matter what my bank account was,
the sort of house I lived in,
or the kind of car I drove ...
but the world may be different because
I was important in the life of a child.

KATHY DAVIS
American Governor (1956–)

On becoming a mother…
I feel whole at last.

MEG MATTHEWS